RAF Jet Bomber Flypast

COVER: A Buccaneer S2 strike aircraft of 12 Squadron from Honington is refuelled in flight by a Victor K1A tanker

PRINTED BY IAN ALLAN PRINTING SHEPPERTON MIDDLESEX TW17 8AN

Philip J. R. Moyes

RAF Jet Bomber Flypast

LONDON
IAN ALLAN LTD

INTRODUCTION

Produced as a companion volume to *RAF Jet Fighter Flypast,* first published in 1972, this book is essentially a collection of 104 photographs, eight of them in colour, illustrating the various types of jet bomber aircraft with which the Royal Air Force has been equipped since the introduction of the Canberra into squadron service in May, 1951. Also included is a machine which did not enter service—the Short Sperrin—yet merits a place in this book because it was designed and built as an insurance against the possible failure of the more ambitious designs which became famous as the V-bombers.

The aircraft are presented chronologically by date of entry into service of the *initial RAF version,* but the various versions and marks of each basic type have been deliberately mixed together. Some reconnaissance, intruder and tanker variants have been included and, as with the earlier volume, the overall aim has been to present an interesting selection of good quality photographs taken from as many angles as possible and at the same time produce a pleasing layout.

It must be stressed that the pictures have been chosen to show, to the best advantage, the aircraft rather than any markings they might carry; and as many Avro and Handley Page negatives are no longer available (the former because of a series of disastrous fires at Manchester some years ago) it is felt that such pictures will be of particular value to enthusiasts and modellers alike.

The photographs come mainly from Industry and Service sources, much assistance being received from Messrs Bill Nutt and R. Wellard of the Ministry of Defence; Alex Johnston, Alec Lumsden and James Oughton of BAC; Mike Byrne, Mike Farlam and John Gray of Hawker Siddeley Aviation; Jim Cownie, Jack Jones and Richard Butcher of Rolls-Royce (1971) Ltd; and Brian Wexham of Vickers Ltd. To them and the many others who have provided pictures for this book, the compiler extends his sincere thanks.—PJRM

First published 1974
ISBN 0 7110 0499 4

All rights reserved. No part of this book may be reproduced or transmitted in any form or by any means, electronic or mechanical, including photocopying, recording or by any information storage and retrieval system, without permission from the Publisher in writing.

© Ian Allan Ltd, 1974

Printed and published in Great Britain by Ian Allan Ltd, Shepperton, Surrey

CONTENTS

English Electric Canberra	5
Vickers Valiant	19
Short Sperrin	32
Colour Plates	33–40
Avro Vulcan	41
Handley Page Victor	50
Hawker Siddeley Buccaneer	59

ENGLISH ELECTRIC CANBERRA

Fourth production Canberra B(I)8 light bomber intruder shows off its ventral gun pack containing four 20-mm cannon as it breaks formation with the camera plane.

Left: Formation of three Canberra B2s of 101 Squadron seen in the winter of 1951/52 on a sortie from Binbrook, Lincs.

Below left: Canberra prototype, VN799, takes off from Warton, near Preston, Lancs, on its first flight, May 13, 1949. Note original rounded fin and rudder.

Right: A B6 of 12 Squadron gets smartly airborne at Hal Far, Malta, for a raid on Egyptian military installation in the Canal Zone during the 1956 Suez Crisis.

Below: Wintry scene at Binbrook 1951/52 when 101 Squadron, first operational squadron to receive Canberras, demonstrated its B2s to the press.

Right: A brand new Canberra B6 pictured during a test flight from Warton. This mark differed from the earlier B2 bomber in having more powerful Rolls-Royce Avon engines, increased tankage and greater range.

Below, right: B6s of 9 Squadron, sporting the unit's famous bat insignia on their fins and Binbrook Wing flashes in red on their noses, prepare for take-off at their snow-covered Lincolnshire base.

Below: Two B(I)6s of 213 Squadron from Bruggen, Germany, pose for the camera in the summer of 1960. Both have the standard B(I)6-type wing stores pylons but only one has the ventral gun pack which was a feature of this interim night intruder version.

FAR LEFT: Piloted by Wg Cdr Roland Beamont, a Canberra B2 is demonstrated to top personnel of the Glenn L Martin Company at Baltimore, Maryland, in 1951, coincidently with a simultaneous announcement that Martin was to build Canberras under licence for the USAF.

LEFT: Three Canberra B6s of 12 Squadron fly in echelon starboard formation during a sortie from their base at Binbrook, Lincs, in September 1958. "Shiny Twelve's" aircraft then had green fins with the fox's mask badge superimposed on a white disc.

BELOW: EX-RAF Canberras pictured at BAC's Salmesbury airfield, near Preston, awaiting refurbishment prior to sale to customers overseas.

Far left: Trio of B16s of 6 Squadron from Akrotiri, Cyprus, early 1962. Each underwing rocket pack carried thirty-seven 2 inch missiles.

Below, left: Canberras were also built, under sub-contract, by Avro, Handley Page and Short Bros. Here the first Avro-built machine, B2 WJ971, is seen on its maiden flight from Woodford, Cheshire, on November 25, 1952, piloted by test pilot J. D. Baker.

Left: A Canberra B6 is loaded with 1 000lb medium capacity bombs. Total internal bomb-load of the Canberra is 6 000lb.

Below: Final assembly of Canberra B2s at English Electric's Warton factory.

Above: Clean lines of the Canberra are emphasised in this head-on view of the first prototype, VN799, piloted by Wg Cdr Roland Beamont.

Below: The Napier Double Scorpion rocket motor test bed Canberra B2 at the Farnborough Air Show in the late 'Fifties. Several machines of this type served with 76 Squadron for atomic cloud sampling during trials in the Pacific of Britain's nuclear weapons.

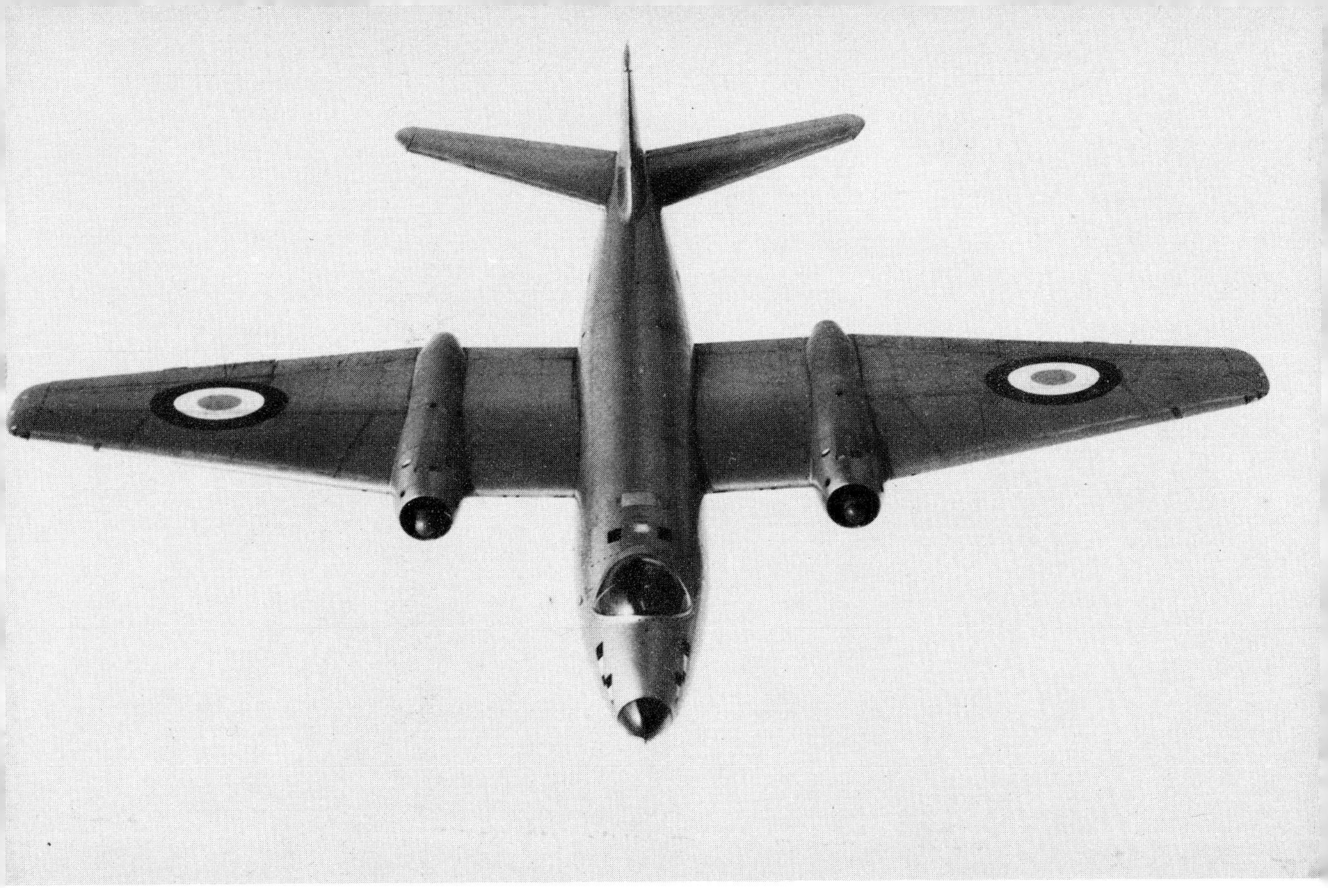

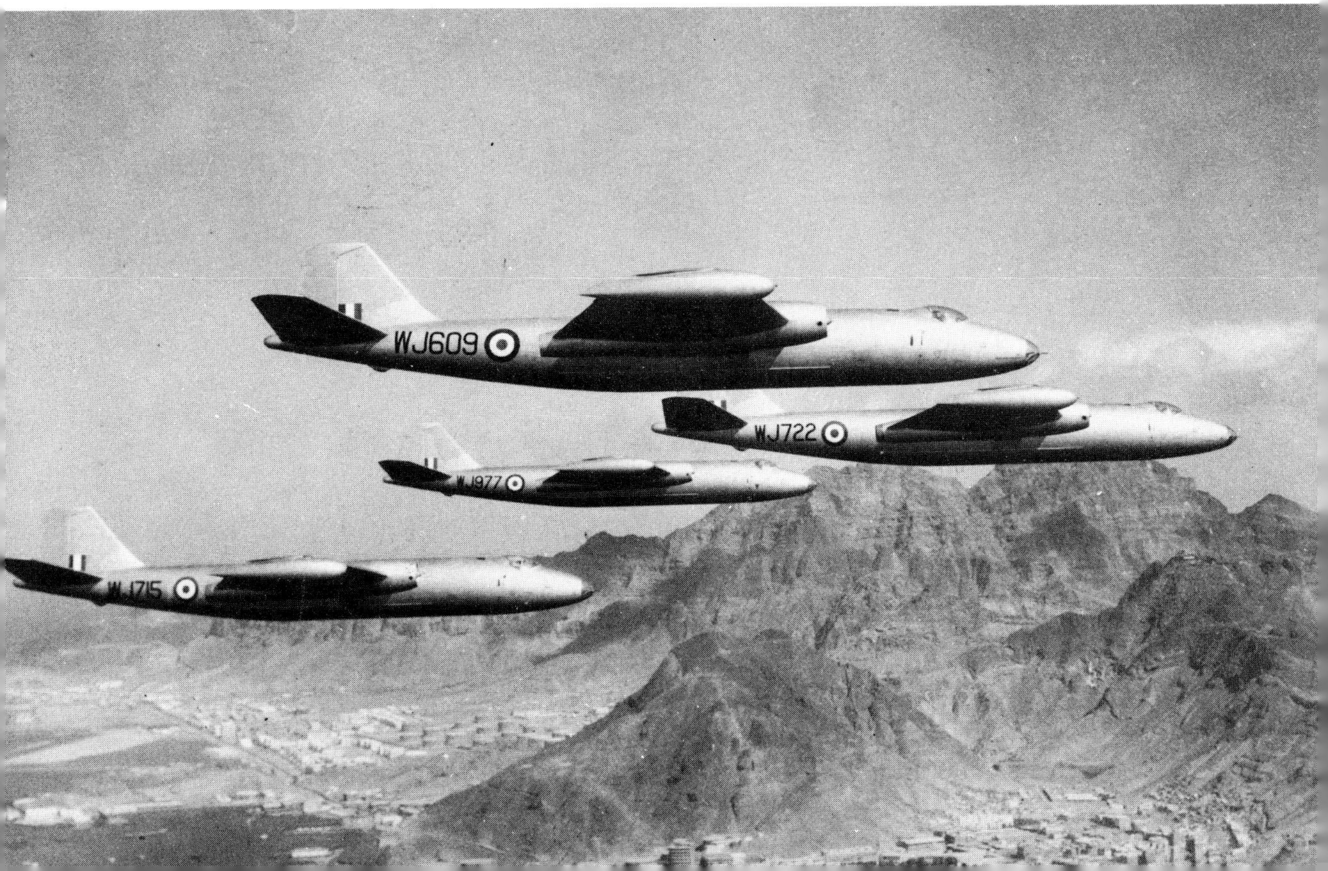
WJ609
WJ722
WJ977
WJ715

Above: A Canberra B15 of 45 Squadron, based at Tengah, Singapore, seen at Chiengmai, Northern, Thailand, during Exercise *Dhanarajata* in 1963.

Right: Ferocious-looking B(I)8 of 16 Squadron at RAF Laarbruch, Germany, in 1972

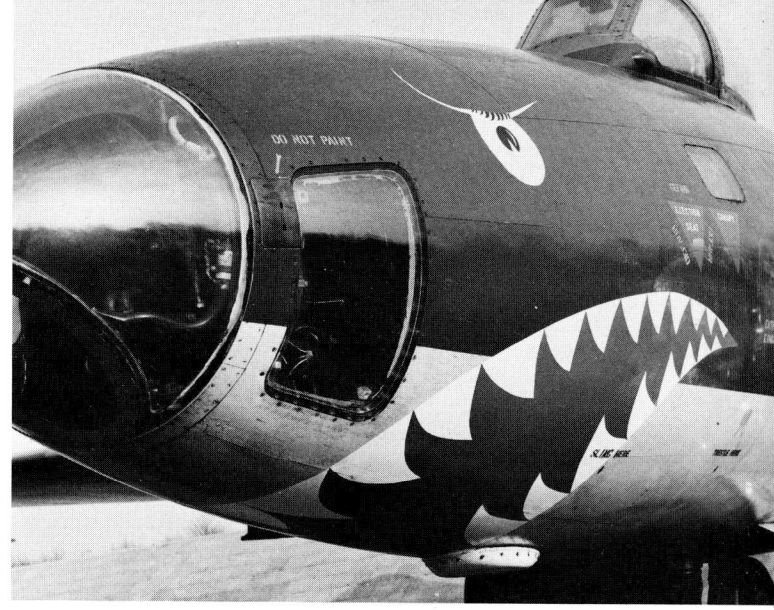

VICKERS VALIANT
A Valiant B(K)1 of 3 Group fitted with long-range wing tanks.

Above: A Valiant B1 (nearest camera) with Mark 1 versions of the RAF's two other types of V bomber, the Vulcan and Victor.

Below: Prototype Valiant (WB210) showing the original narrow slot-type intakes.

Above: Valiant BK1 with nose probe for flight refuelling.

Below: A B(PR)1 in the camouflage introduced shortly before all Valiants were grounded because of metal fatigue problems in December 1964.

Facing page: A fine study of XD823, taken over the sea.

Above: A crew scramble to their aircraft at Wyton, Hunts, during a visit to the station by HRH Prince Philip, Duke of Edinburgh, in June 1958.

Below: Final production Valiant, XD875, takes off from Brooklands for delivery to the RAF on August 27, 1957.

Left: Close up of a B(K)1 fitted with overload tanks. Ventral nose blister housed the bomb-aimer.

Below, left: This B1, WP204, was used to test the Avro Blue Steel stand-off bomb.

Below: A view of the 'Black Bomber', the prototype Valiant B2. Distinctive features were the underslung pods into which the bogie undercarriage retracted backwards.

Above: A Valiant PR(K)1 of 543 Squadron formating with a Canberra PR9 and a PR7 from 58 Squadron, Wyton, in November 1961.

Above, right: Night servicing scene featuring a Valiant of 'B' Flight, Wittering, October 1956.

Far right: Sole example of the B2 prototype which was designed for low-level pathfinding and nicknamed the 'black bomber' because of its night paint. It did not enter RAF service.

Right: Service Chief gives starting instructions to a Valiant captain through outside intercomm at Wittering in August 1956.

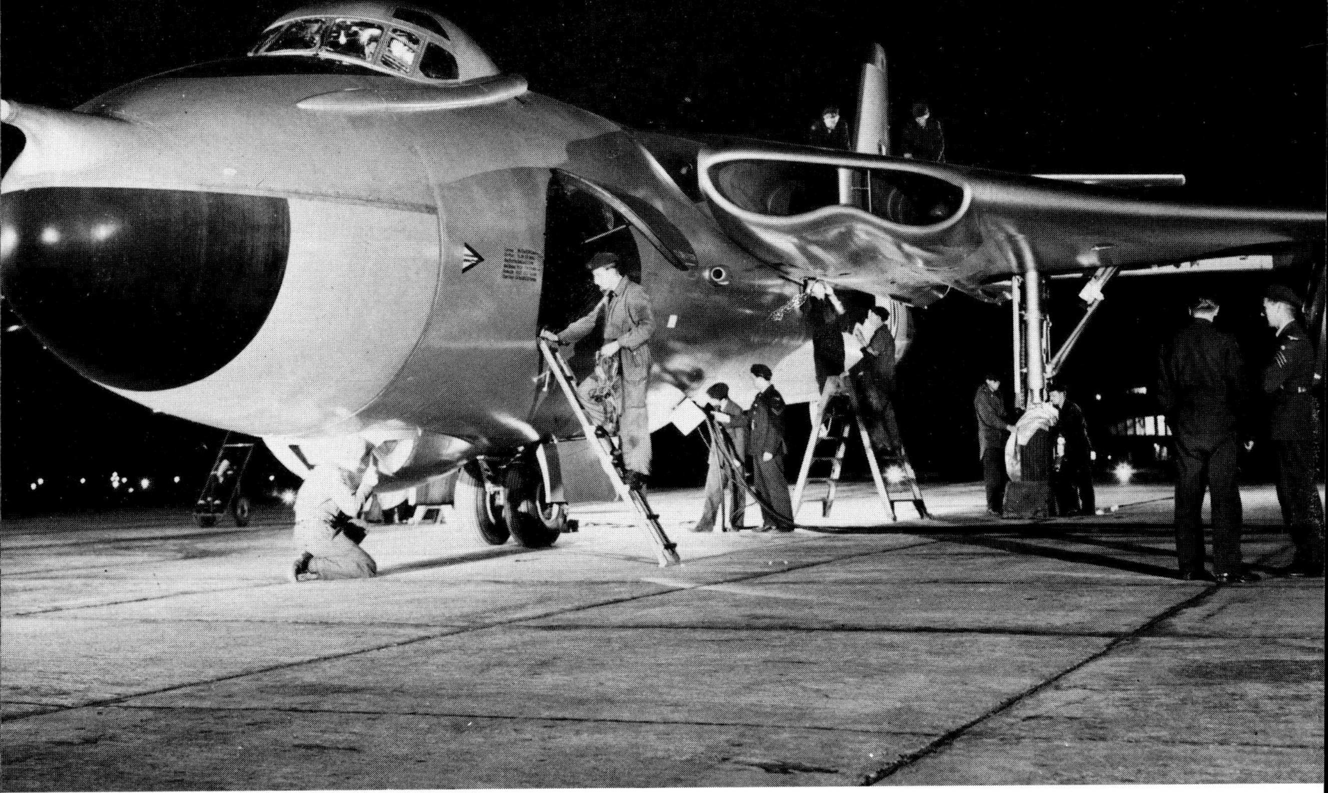

Left: A Valiant tanker fitted with long range tanks refuells a receiver Valiant.

Below, left: One of the two twin Valiant production lines at Weybridge. The Valiant was the first of the 'V' Class four-jet bombers to enter RAF squadron service.

Right: Valiants of 138 Squadron at Gaydon, Hunts, which re-formed in January 1955, was the first squadron of Bomber Command to receive the type.

Below: Another study of a newly camouflaged Valiant B(K)1. This finish was introduced for all V-bombers when they assumed a low-level role early in 1964.

Facing page: Yet another camera angle on B(K)1 XD823. A machine from the same production batch, XD818, dropped Britain's first H bomb, at Christmas Island, on May 15, 1957.

Above: B(PR)K1 WZ395 of 148 Squadron scrambles during a demonstration at the Farnborough Air Show.

Below: Another Farnborough Show occasion—ten Valiants of 138 Squadron lined up before making a formation flight.

SHORT SPERRIN

Although it did not enter RAF service the Short Sperrin merits inclusion in this book as it was designed and built as an insurance against the failure of the more ambitious V-bombers. It was less advanced aerodynamically than the Valiant, Vulcan and Victor and two prototypes were built and flown, VX158 and '161.

Canberra B2 of RAF Strike Command serving in a training role in 1973.

Generally similar to the Canberra bomber is the Canberra T4 dual control trainer which entered service in 1954. This example, from 231 OCU, RAF Cottesmore, was photographed as recently as February, 1973.

Valiant of 214 (tanker) Squadron photographed on take-off from Wisley.

Vulcan B2, armed with a Blue Steel stand-off bomb, over the Niagara Falls.

A Blue Steel-carrying Vulcan B2 is serviced prior to a night exercise.

Vulcan B2 of the NEAF Bomber Wing over Cyprus in 1973.

Victor B1 in the white, anti-flash finish once adopted by Bomber Command's V-bomber force.

Buccaneer S2 of 237 OCU, Honington, carrying underwing rocket pods.

AVRO VULCAN

A Vulcan of 617 Squadron on a sortie from Scampton, Lincs, carrying a Blue Steel stand-off bomb.

Right: A B2 of the NEAF Bomber Wing, sporting type B roundels and fin flashes, on a sortie from Akrotiri, Cyprus, in February 1973.

Below, right: Dramatic take-off study of a Blue Steel-carrying Vulcan B2.

Below: Second prototype Vulcan deploys its brake parachute at the 1957 Farnborough Air Show.

A Vulcan B2 carrying two Douglas Skybolt aerodynamic test vehicles. The Skybolt air-launched ballistic missile development programme was cancelled in 1962 in favour of the submarine-launched Polaris.

Right: A B2, in the high gloss camouflage introduced in 1964 for low-level operations, armed with the Blue Steel.

Below: A B2 of Strike Command undergoes a maintenance check at its dispersal before a night sortie.

Above: Second prototype Vulcan, VX777, showing to advantage the type's original delta planform with straight swept leading edges.

Below: A B2 of the NEAF Bomber Wing takes off past a Lightning of 23 Squadron at Akotiri in November 1972.

Right: B2 XM599 releases its full 'conventional' load of 21 1 000lb bombs in salvo.

Far right: Vulcan B2s at Tengah, Singapore, during a visit to the Far East.

Below: A Vulcan B2 formates with a Spitfire 14 over RAF Finningley, Yorks, in 1968.

HANDLEY PAGE VICTOR

A Victor B1 of 10 Squadron—first squadron equipped with the Handley page crescent-wing bomber—demonstrates its air brakes during a sortie from Cottesmore, Rutland, in 1958.

Above: A B2BS (or B2R as the type was also known), in camouflage for low-level penetrations, carrying an Avro Blue Steel stand-off bomb.

Below: A K1A three-point tanker of 57 squadron is pursued by two thirsty customers, a Buccaneer and a Phantom.

Right: A Victor B1 from A&AEE, Boscombe Down, is refuelled by a USAF KB-50J during compatability trials in 1961.

Facing page, top to bottom: Shark-like Blue Steel stand-off bomb beneath a Victor B2 test platform in late 1961.

A K1A of 57 Squadron deploys its brake parachute on landing.

Prototype Victor, WB771, which first flew on December 24, 1952, at Boscombe Down, seen in its original natural metal finish.

Below: A B1 of 15 Squadron is marshalled in at Cottesmore after a night sortie in December 1958.

Above: SR2 XL161 of 543 Squadron streams its brake parachute after touching down. Note Kuchemann "carrots"—aerodynamic modifications—on wings.

Below: Blue Steel training round is manhandled under the belly of a Victor B2BS of 139 (Jamaica) Squadron at Wittering. Note ECM "warts" around Victor's tail cone.

B1 XA930 flying in August 1958 with large auxiliary underwing tanks and the prototype FR probe installation.

XA930 was previously used for RATOG trials with two DH Sprites carried in underwing packs.

Below: A 55 Squadron Victor K1A tanker refuells a CAF CF-5A during trials from RAF Marham, Norfolk.

Left, top to bottom:
A Victor B2 on test from Radlett. First operational unit to receive the type was 139 Squadron at Wittering in February 1962.

XL231, first Victor to be converted by Hawker Siddeley to a K2 tanker, on test from HSA's Woodford facility early in 1972.

Another view of the prototype Victor B1 in its 1953 SBAC Display paint scheme.

Below: A B1A of 15 Squadron drops its full "conventional" load of 35 x 1 000lb bombs at Song Song Range in 1964.

Vic of Victor B1s of 15 Squadron on a sortie from Cottesmore.

HAWKER SIDDELEY BUCCANEER

A Buccaneer S2 armed with 10 000lb of bombs streaks across RAF Elvington airfield, near York, during heavy load handling trials in 1972.

Above: A Buccaneer S2 carrying the unique Roman style numerals of 15 Squadron takes off from its base at Laarbruch on the Dutch/German border.

Below: S2s of 12 Squadron, sporting the unit's famous fox's mask badge on the engine air intakes, lined up at Honington, Suffolk.

Above right: Four Buccaneers of 12 Squadron in echelon port formation. This unit was the first RAF Squadron to receive the Buccaneer—at Honington in October 1969.

Right: An S2 armed with Martel missiles is catapulted from HMS *Ark Royal* during deck trials.

Above: Fat and folded An aircraft of 12 Squadron in B type national insignia at Decimomannu, Sardinia, in 1972.

Below: RAF Buccaneers can carry an additional bomb door fuel tank which increases the normal internal capacity by 425 without any loss in weapon carriage capability.

Above: An S2 shows off its load of four Martel missiles during trials at Hawker Siddeley's test airfield at Holme-on-Spalding Moor, Yorks.

Below: The black and gold insignia of 16 Squadron are displayed by this machine photographed at Laarbruch, Germany, in 1973 when the squadron was working up on the type.

Above: An S2 of 12 Squadron fires a salvo of 68 mm SNEB rockets during armament practice in December 1972.

Below: A Buccaneer carrying twelve 1 000 bombs on the wing pylons. In addition a further four 1 000 bombs can be carried internally in the rotating bomb bay, giving a total weapon load of 16 000 lb.